Original title:
You and Me in Every Lifetime

Copyright © 2024 Creative Arts Management OÜ
All rights reserved.

Author: Adam Phillips
ISBN HARDBACK: 978-9908-0-0898-1
ISBN PAPERBACK: 978-9908-0-0899-8

Embracing Yesterday's Ghosts

In each old photo, we both smile,
Haunting the past, just for a while.
Dressed like clowns in a black-and-white,
Making mischief in the pale moonlight.

Chasing shadows that dance in the air,
While we giggle at ghosts without care.
Turning back time with a wink and a grin,
Who knew being silly could be our win?

Twin Flames Through Centuries

Two candles flicker through time's long roll,
Warming up tales, igniting the soul.
In silly wigs and outrageous hats,
Creating chuckles where there were spats.

Time travelers lost, but never to fret,
Spilling our drinks, placing our bets.
From ancient feasts to modern cafes,
Finding the fun in all of our plays.

The Unbroken Circle

Round and round, we spin like tops,
Giggling as each memory flops.
In a polka-dot world, we prance and dance,
Giving gray days a colorful chance.

A merry-go-round of laughter and glee,
We're a duo that's far from a spree.
Making our mark in a comical twist,
In the circle of life, we've got it all kissed.

Twin Flames Through Centuries

Two candles flicker through time's long roll,
Warming up tales, igniting the soul.
In silly wigs and outrageous hats,
Creating chuckles where there were spats.

Time travelers lost, but never to fret,
Spilling our drinks, placing our bets.
From ancient feasts to modern cafes,
Finding the fun in all of our plays.

The Unbroken Circle

Round and round, we spin like tops,
Giggling as each memory flops.
In a polka-dot world, we prance and dance,
Giving gray days a colorful chance.

A merry-go-round of laughter and glee,
We're a duo that's far from a spree.
Making our mark in a comical twist,
In the circle of life, we've got it all kissed.

Inked in the Stars

Under a sky of twinkling light,
Drawing doodles till late at night.
Constellations don't take themselves too serious,
Even the comets are quite delirious.

We scribble stories on celestial pages,
As the universe chuckles through ages.
With every wink from a shimmering star,
We laugh at life, no matter how far.

For All the Times to Come

In a world of swirling shades,
We stumble, trip, and roll,
Wacky fates we can't evade,
Like socks lost in a hole.

From cavemen with their clubs,
To queens with shiny crowns,
We dance through life with shrugs,
And wear each other's frowns.

On pirate ships we shout,
With parrots on our heads,
Even through the stormy doubt,
We'll share our soggy breads.

Through every tick of time,
Our quirks will intertwine,
In cosmic jest, sublime,
Like grapes that twist and twine.

In the Afterglow of Ages

In fragrances of yore,
We plot and scheme with glee,
In castles made of ore,
We share old cheese and tea.

From knights in shining mail,
To wizards with their wands,
Our mischief sets the sail,
Run wild in various ponds.

With laughter, we embark,
On quests of shoe-tying,
Adventure's tasty spark,
While dragons keep on frying.

In twilight's cheeky light,
With shadows on parade,
Our spirits take flight,
In every grand charade.

The Chronicle of Our Souls

In dusty books of lore,
Our tales are etched in ink,
Like old socks in a drawer,
We giggle, roast, and wink.

From outer space to earth,
We're stars in drag and gowns,
With humor for our worth,
And gags that flip and frown.

Through epochs vast and wide,
We juggle and we fall,
With history as our ride,
For laughs we have it all.

Like bubbles in the stream,
We bounce and pop with flair,
In laughter's endless dream,
Our souls have not a care.

Infinite Harmonies

In symphonies of time,
We orchestrate the prank,
With beats that bend and climb,
   Our tune a rolling tank.

From flutes of feathered birds,
To drums made out of pies,
We dance beyond absurd,
With giggles as our ties.

With rhythms that entice,
We sway from here to there,
In vibrant sound so nice,
We'll make the world our fair.

In every note and beat,
Our laughter we will weave,
Creating something sweet,
   To share and to believe.

Eternal Echoes of Us

In a world where cows wear shoes,
I trip on shoelaces, sing the blues.
Through wormholes we jump and play,
Finding lost socks in a time delay.

With jello molds and silly hats,
We dance with cats and chat with bats.
A tickle fight in a pancake span,
We flip our worries, yes we can!

Under disco balls and neon lights,
We plan heists on cookie nights.
Eating doughnuts in flight,
This quirky love feels just right.

Threads of Time Intertwined

In every age, you're still a clown,
Inventing shoes that turn us round.
As knights, we juggle sword and shield,
In silly wars, we refuse to yield.

From cavemen painting on the wall,
To tweeting goats that dance and ball,
We crack jokes in the stone-age style,
Time's a prank—let's stay a while!

In spaceships we choose donut holes,
As aliens, we dance like shoals.
With every travel round and round,
Our laughter in infinity is found.

Remnants of a Shared Soul

In a galaxy of mismatched shoes,
We play hopscotch with cosmic blues.
With chicken hats and pogo sticks,
We find our joy among the quips.

Through history's zany, wild mist,
We laugh at the things that we've missed.
As pirates, we steal rubber ducks,
In every lifetime, well, what the muck?

Time travelers on a scooter spree,
Baking cookies in zero-G.
We're two peas in a nutty pod,
With laughter echoing like a god.

Weaving Through Infinity

In realms where toast shops float on high,
We taste the clouds and learn to fly.
Dancing on stilts down memory lane,
Wearing our quirks like a bright campaign.

With rubber chickens and bubble gum,
We write love notes to the sunflower's drum.
A race with turtles, we take a dip,
Time's quirky prankster on a cosmic trip.

In every tick of the cosmic clock,
We build our dreams made of silly rock.
Through mischief and giggles, we continue to play,
In a tapestry woven, come what may!

From Dawn to Dusk, Again

When the sun peeks in, we hop out of bed,
With mismatched socks and a laugh in our head.
We dance in the kitchen, all wobbly and bright,
Coffee spills laughing, oh, what a sight!

Off to the market, we prance like two fools,
Buying odd snacks and the craziest tools.
The cart's like a ship, sailing seas of delight,
As we battle the snacks in a candy canapé fight.

Later we wander, down paths full of cheer,
Stepping on cracks, making trouble appear.
We trip over laughter, roll on the grass,
As the sun paints our frames, time slips like glass.

Now twilight arrives with a wink and a nod,
We share silly tales, like we're cousins or gods.
With the stars as our witnesses, we giggle and sigh,
Chasing fireflies' dances, oh, how time can fly!

Conversations Beyond Existence

In the realm where ghosts meet grins,
We chat while juggling shimmery sins.
Do you recall that silly hat?
I wore it once while chasing a cat.

The stars giggle at our silly fights,
Arguing over who gets the first bites.
But in every jest and every prank,
Our laughter echoes; it's a cosmic bank.

Upon the clouds, we smile and snipe,
You calling me out for my terrible type.
I trip on stardust, oh what a scene!
Yet in this chaos, we reign as the green.

So with every poke and playful tease,
We weave our tales like a gentle breeze.
Who knew the afterlife was so bright?
We banter and play in the endless night.

The Dance of the Ages

In a ballroom made of swirling time,
We twirl and stumble, oh what a rhyme!
You step on my toes, and I let out a squeal,
In this ancient waltz, we spin with zeal.

The flapper days and disco nights,
We groove like legends in outlandish tights.
With every misstep, we laugh, we glance,
This cosmic twist is an endless dance.

Once a knight, you dropped your sword,
A bard of mischief, I struck a chord.
In every era, we're quite the pair,
Strutting through history with flamboyant flair.

The music fades, but not our cheer,
In every decade, we reappear.
From palaces to park benches, we sway,
Life is a party; come join the fray!

Threads of Love through Time

In a tapestry woven with giggles and glee,
We stitch our moments, just you and me.
With needle and thread, we patch up the past,
Each quirk a reminder; we sure had a blast.

Stitches from centuries, bright and bold,
You knitted a scarf; oh, that's pure gold!
While I tried weaving in clumsy designs,
This fabric of time forever entwines.

From stone ages to the digital buzz,
Our laughter threads through, as true love does.
I found the yarn in the skies so blue,
Wrapping our moments like a crazy glue.

Yet as the world spins and colors unwind,
Our playful threads tie moments unconfined.
For every loop of fate, I wear it proud,
In this bizarre quilt, we're forever loud!

Undying in Every Form

Reborn as squirrels, we scamper and tease,
Chasing each other through the autumn trees.
In our furry hands, acorns we've got,
But you take the biggest; oh, what a plot!

Next life we're fish in a shimmering stream,
Splashing around like it's a wild dream.
You splash me first, then pretend to glide,
In this aquatic game, we let love ride.

From towering trees to depths below,
In every shape, our antics still flow.
One life as stars, a shimmer in flight,
Together we giggle in the velvet night.

With every transformation, we're bound to find,
The joy in our journeys, truly undefined.
From furry to finned, our spirit is clear,
In every form, it's laughter we wear!

Where Time Knows No Bounds

In every era, a curious dance,
An awkward shuffle, a clown's chance.
In the past, we wore powdered wigs,
Now we're here with silly digs.

In pyramids or castles grand,
We'd drop each other's ice cream, then stand.
Planning grand heists with feathered hats,
While not forgetting to trip on mats.

From ancient scripts to memes so bold,
Our stories echo, but oh, so troll'd.
Each mishap shared, a laugh that's loud,
In every age, we're a goofy crowd.

So here's to us, through thick and thin,
With every giggle, we surely win.
Through every wrinkle of space and time,
We'll keep on laughing, our silliest rhyme.

The Legacy of Our Connection.

From the dawn of time, a jest was spun,
Two quirky souls, always having fun.
In every epoch, a prank we'd pull,
As history whispers, we're never dull.

In caveman days, we'd hunt for fire,
Then trip on rocks, and roll in the mire.
Fast forward to space, we're astronauts,
Still bickering over the last donut spots.

With every invention, our antics grow,
From drawing on walls to TikTok shows.
Each lifetime's a circus, with you as the clown,
In the grand scheme, we both wear the crown.

So cheers to the future, and all that's ahead,
Where we'll giggle together, never misled.
Through time's goofy tunnel, hand in hand,
Forever your fool, in this whimsical land.

Eternal Echoes of Us

In Rome, we sat, throwing bread at ducks,
In medieval gowns, we pulled all the plucks.
Across centuries, we caused quite a scene,
A chuckle each age, we're the comic routine.

In pirate ships, we'd sing off-key,
While stealing gold, you'd stick it on me.
Past raucous duels and whispered plans,
We'd still misplace our own treasure scans.

From Victorian balls to future's spree,
Our legacy's laughter, the key to be free.
In every cycle, we dance and we spin,
In this wacky timeline, let the giggles begin!

So here's to our echoes, forever in play,
In this merry loop, we'll frolic each day.
Through every echo that time can bestow,
We'll laugh through the ages, our delight ever glow.

Whispers Across Timelines

In flickering lights or lanterns bold,
Our whispers travel, sly and old.
From carriages to flying machines,
Our witty exchanges remain evergreen.

In every timeline, we plot our schemes,
From silly dreams to outrageous memes.
We're pirates, kings, or just two pals,
In every chapter, we reign as gals.

With a wink, a grin, and a cheeky tease,
Our cosmic joke brings the universe to its knees.
Through jest and jive, we'll never part,
For timeless laughter is the heart's best art.

So let's raise a toast, wherever we might land,
For giggles and joys that are perfectly planned.
As timelines twist, our spirits will soar,
With every chuckle, we're bound evermore.

Memories Beyond the Veil

In each life, we bumble around,
Like two lost socks on the ground.
You steal my fries, I roll my eyes,
Yet we laugh until we cry.

In another time, I wore a hat,
And you chased squirrels, how about that?
With every scheme that went awry,
We still find ways to fly high.

From board games to bad karaoke,
We make the mundane quite zany.
When we trip over our own two feet,
It's a dance that none can beat!

So raise a toast to all those days,
In every life, through various ways.
Let's keep this laughter as our tale,
And cherish whims beyond the veil.

Timeless Bond of Two Spirits

In each old tale, we find the fun,
You eat the cake, I just run.
Like ghosts that prank, we never quit,
Causing mischief, we'll never sit.

Past lives had us, both in hats,
With rubber chickens and silly spats.
We'd hold our sides, from laughing hard,
As we danced in a backyard yard.

Whether kings or clowns, we wear a smile,
Playing hopscotch across each mile.
With every blooper, every jest,
This timeless bond, we are so blessed.

So if I'm lost, just shout my name,
Like a cartoon, I'll pop up, same!
In every age, we find our spark,
You crack a joke, I'll light the dark.

Always Returning to Home

From pyramids to pirate ships,
We've sailed the seas and had some flips.
With treasure maps and goofy hats,
We've won the day against all odds.

In every home, we've made a mess,
With cereal spills, we take no stress.
You've made me think, I'm quite a hoot,
Your antics give my heart a root.

Past gardens grew a million flowers,
But we just chased the fleeting hours.
With laughter echoing through the trees,
We find our way upon the breeze.

Returning back, to silly dreams,
We stitch our souls at the seams.
And when the clock strikes laugh o'clock,
Home is where we share the shock!

Resonance in Every Heartbeat

Your giggles ripple through the air,
Like bubbles floating without a care.
In every beat, we find the rhyme,
Bouncing through the sands of time.

From pranks we pulled in a brief past,
To silly cheers that echo vast.
Who knew two goofballs could align,
With every giggle, every sign?

We're echoes of each other's glee,
Like two dandelions on the spree.
In every sketch or silly charade,
We dance to tunes that life has made.

So should we fall through time once more,
Let's chase rainbows and laugh galore.
With every heartbeat, loud and free,
We create our own harmony.

Songs of the Undying

In every age, we dance and twirl,
Like clumsy ducks in a grand old swirl.
You steal the last bite of my pie,
I chase you down with a "Don't even try!"

Through storms and calm, we seem to find,
Each other's quirks, forever entwined.
Like socks that vanish in the wash,
We always find a way to squash!

Serendipity in Every Era

From pyramids to neon lights,
We bumble through, what a silly sight!
In every life, you're clueless as a bee,
Buzzing 'round saying, "Is that cake for me?"

A Roman feast or a wild cowboy show,
You trip on your spurs, oh what a blow!
Still laughing hard as the world does spin,
In every turn, it's a goofy win.

Souls Entwined Forevermore

Through thick and thin, our fates collide,
From courtroom trials to a rollercoaster ride.
You may swipe left, but I'll still insist,
A connection like ours is hard to resist!

In each era, our laughter's the key,
Like clowns on a tightrope, we sail so free.
With pies in our faces and jokes on demand,
Who knew forever could be so unplanned?

Destined to Meet Again

In every twist, we jest and jibe,
From past lives with a quirk-filled vibe.
Each encounter, a slapstick spree,
"Wait, are you that guy from 173?"

In medieval halls or future's bright glow,
We're tossing confetti, stealing the show.
No time apart, just giggles and glee,
In the grand cosmic plan, who wouldn't agree?

Fragments of Our Forever

In every role, I play a fool,
You laugh at me, and that's the rule.
From kings to jesters, we won't tire,
Chasing giggles, fueled by fire.

In past lives, I wore a crown,
You were a bird, I chased around.
Now in this scene, a taco truck,
Dancing away, we're out of luck.

Cast as pirates, sailing the high seas,
Finding treasure, with the greatest ease.
Yet all we find are socks and crumbs,
In this wild chase, we're such silly bums.

Through all the jokes and silly plots,
We'll keep on laughing, tie the knots.
In every age, we stick like glue,
Forever puzzled, just me and you.

Guardians of the Same Star

In every era, what a pair,
You've been my monster, my big ol' bear.
With capes and masks, we fight for fun,
While avoiding chores, we still have won.

In a past life, you were a cat,
Me the dog, imagine that!
Chasing tails in a psychedelic dream,
Always plotting our next scheme.

Astrologers might call it fate,
But we just laugh at our own state.
With silly dances and awkward sighs,
We'll twirl beneath the starlit skies.

Whatever form we take, I swear,
Our joy will always fill the air.
Guardians of laughter, come what may,
We'll keep it goofy every day.

Reflections Across the Ages

In haunted halls and castles grand,
You're the ghost who won't understand.
I trip on stairs, you float with grace,
In every dream, we share this space.

Through history's books, we take a peek,
I shout for bread, you call for cheek.
In taverns loud, we toast our fate,
Swapping stories 'til it's late.

From mimes to minstrels, we've played them all,
Every character, we have a ball.
But in the end, we're quite absurd,
Words from our lips, just mumbling blurb.

In every time, it's always clear,
We keep our laughter ever near.
Reflections dance, with glee we'll sing,
Two silly souls, it's a wondrous thing.

Shadows of Us in the Moonlight

Beneath the moon, we make our plan,
With shadows dancing, hand in hand.
You steal my fries, that sneaky thief,
Yet I must laugh, despite my grief.

In a past life, we were coyotes wild,
Chasing echoes, I was the child.
Howling laughter through the night,
A serenade of pure delight.

With a wink and grin, we chase the moon,
Flipping shadows like a cartoon.
In every form, we've made a ruckus,
Finding joy in all that's circus.

Through thick and thin, with winks and quirks,
Our bond survives, no need for works.
In every glow, we're out to play,
Two funny specters, come what may.

A Love Beyond Measure

In a world where socks go missing,
We find our pairs, still kissing.
Lost keys lead us on a chase,
But laughter wins the silly race.

Through burnt pancakes and wobbly chairs,
We dance around without a care.
Our quirky ways, they keep us bright,
Like glitter in the dark of night.

With every blunder, every fall,
You crack a joke; we both stand tall.
Building castles out of air,
Who knew love was so rarefare?

Our wacky tales etched in time,
Every silly prank, a rhyme.
In this circus, we wear the crowns,
With laughter echoing through the towns.

Tales Written in the Cosmos

Under stars that wink and twinkle,
You swear you saw a shooting sprinkle.
I laugh and say it's just your charm,
No need for space to keep us warm.

In galaxies where giggles land,
We hold our joy with sticky hands.
Aliens envy our mundane joys,
When we playfight like silly boys.

Teleporting snacks from fridge to plate,
Our laughter echoes, oh so great!
Cosmic love with a pinch of fun,
Every day feels like a run.

So let's defy the heavy laws,
With laughter as our cosmic cause.
In the universe, we'll weave our tale,
Of silly dreams that shall not fail.

The Legacy of Our Bond

In history books, we're quite the pair,
With stories only we can share.
Our cozy chaos, a sweet delight,
Like chocolate fondue in moonlight.

Through ancient lands of bread and cheese,
We twirl around with such great ease.
Inventing dances, odd and bold,
Our legacy is laughter told.

Mismatched socks and fridge art too,
Add colors to our view askew.
A tapestry of jokes we weave,
In this bond, we truly believe.

Let history forget the boring prose,
For our love, only laughter grows.
In every giggle, we've made our mark,
Living legends in our lucky park.

When Worlds Collide

When planets clash, they make a show,
Like when we trip in the grocery flow.
Carts collide with hilarious sound,
As we laugh, our joy's unbound.

With spaceships made of pizza boxes,
We blast off while dodging hypoxic foxes.
Gravity fails but our spirits soar,
In this world, we forever adore.

Our jokes are like meteors bright,
Lighting up the canvas of night.
As worlds collide, in cosmic cheer,
We find our home, forever near.

So let the comets race and glide,
We're the stars with nowhere to hide.
In this universe, we are the spark,
Creating laughter, leaving a mark.

Love's Infinite Refrain

In every age, we find a game,
With goofy hats and silly names.
We dance like fools in a moonlit glow,
Two jesters lost in a timeless flow.

From ancient Rome to future skies,
We tumble through each sweet surprise.
With every laugh, a bond we weave,
In quirky tales, we both believe.

A wink, a grin, we take our chance,
In the oddest moments, we love to prance.
With rubber chickens and confetti too,
Each footstep sings, "I still choose you!"

So grab a snack and spin around,
In this theater, joy is found.
For in every jibe, a truth remains,
A laugh echoes through love's refrains.

Threads of Destiny Woven

In every thread that fate has spun,
We stitch a life of quirky fun.
With mismatched socks and wobbly chairs,
Our tapestry grows through silly fares.

In ancient times, we shared a pie,
You tossed a slice, oh me, oh my!
With every bite, a history made,
Our spirits dance like confetti laid.

We roam the past in cartoon suits,
Playing hopscotch in our goofy boots.
No matter the year, from frowns to cheer,
We weave the threads of love, so dear.

With yarn and laughter, we can't go wrong,
A cozy quilt where both belong.
In every weave, our love's displayed,
Silly and sweet, it's perfectly made.

Through Ages, Hand in Hand

From dinosaurs to flying cars,
We've traveled far beneath the stars.
In cardboard ships, we sail the seas,
Chasing seagulls, collecting breeze.

When ancient knights wore polka dots,
We jousted close, dodging frying pots.
In every clash, we'd laugh and shout,
"Who knew love meant a silly bout?"

We've flown on broomsticks, danced with gnomes,
In forests filled with whimsical homes.
Through time we twirl with clumsy glee,
Two clowns embracing eternity.

So here's to us, a comical pair,
Hand in hand, we've built the rare.
Through every time, our spirits play,
In absurd bliss, we find our way.

Heartbeats in the Sand

On sunlit shores where waves collide,
We strolled with flip-flops, side by side.
With every splash, a giggle shared,
In silly shorts, we never cared.

We drew our dreams in the golden grains,
With castles tall and funny names.
Our heartbeats danced with ocean tunes,
As seabirds laughed beneath the moons.

In sandcastles that surely fell,
We'd yell, "Oops!" and build a shell.
With every tide, a new delight,
We play like kids from day to night.

So here we sit, with grains of fate,
Creating fun as we can't wait.
In every grain, our joys expand,
A funny love, forever planned.

Constellations We Create

In every diner booth, we plot our stars,
As we share fries and dream of Mars.
Your laugh is the comet, bright and loud,
Together we orbit, no need for a crowd.

With ketchup conspiracies and cola spills,
We sketch the cosmos, ignoring the thrills.
Your silly theories make me roll my eyes,
But who could resist such a fun surprise?

Every spilled drink is a supernova,
As we joke about aliens who need a do-over.
We're the astronauts in our home-made craft,
Navigating laughter, in our silly gaffe.

In the galaxy of goofy, we lead the way,
Chasing down meteors at the end of the day.
Among the stars, let the mischief ignite,
For every lifetime, we'll keep it light.

Memories Bound by Time

A calendar flipped brings a chuckle or two,
Those old-fashioned photos, what were we in to?
Wearing those outfits that defy all trends,
With hairdos like clouds, where the silliness blends.

We reminisce fondly about joys and the flops,
Filling the air with our laughter that hops.
Every detail teased is a treasure we keep,
From shoes that were trendy to secrets so deep.

Time travelers, we are, in our own bizarre way,
Revisiting moments that brightened our day.
With pasts we poke fun at, we dance and we spin,
In the memory factory, we always win.

Running down memory lanes, we trip and we fall,
But giggles will catch us, we'll stand proud and tall.
Linked by our quirks and shared tales of delight,
Who could have guessed friendship would take such flight?

Chasing Shadows of the Past

In the attic of time, we find our old toys,
Dusty memories whisper, turn into a noise.
Your goofy old puppet just can't stop the show,
As shadows dance wildly, putting on a glow.

We chase down the echoes that make us both grin,
With mischief and laughter, let the games begin!
Bouncing off walls with nostalgia's sweet weight,
Who knew old sunlight could summon such fate?

Those awkward first crushes, oh, what a scene,
Fumbling with feelings that felt just like green.
We reenact moments, and giggle 'til dawn,
In the chase of our shadows, the ages are gone.

With each silly step, the past starts to sway,
Our laughter cuts through it, keeping shadows at bay.
As we uncover tales that were lost in the glow,
In the storybook of us, we thrive on the show.

A Dance Beyond the Ages

In a ballroom of laughter, we sway and we spin,
With goofy old moves, let the games begin.
Your two left feet make the floor a delight,
As we trip through the centuries, hearts holding tight.

Our dance is a stamp on time's swirling page,
With the rhythm of giggles, we burst from the cage.
Waltzing through history, what steps will we take?
With each clumsy twirl, oh, the laughter we make!

In costumes of chaos, we twinkle and shout,
Each era we hop brings a new fun route.
The jester's come calling, inviting us near,
As we dance down the ages, spreading out cheer.

With hearts intertwined, we shimmy and sway,
Two stars in the cosmos, come laugh, join the play.
Through all of the ages, our joy won't cease,
In this cosmic dance, we find our sweet peace.

Starlit Promises

Under the sky, we dance and twirl,
In silly hats that make us whirl.
We laugh at fate, like kids in play,
Chasing the stars that lead the way.

In past lives, you were a cat,
And I a mouse, imagine that!
We'd run in circles, laugh and shout,
Drawing the cosmos' playful route.

Our quirks a thread through time's great loom,
Painting our tales in cosmic bloom.
A clown in every tale we weave,
Together in pranks, we never leave.

So here's to us in every jest,
In socks and sandals, poorly dressed.
From fox and hound to stars so bright,
We'll keep on laughing, day and night.

Through the Sands of Rebirth

In deserts bare, we lose our way,
Past lives blend in a comical play.
You were a queen, I served your tea,
And you said, 'Oh, this isn't free!'

In Egypt, we built a silly pyramid,
Baking cupcakes, who knew we'd did?
Pharaohs laugh at our odd design,
Sands shift, but our fun's divine.

From turtles racing across the shore,
To pizza makers, let's make more!
In every laugh, the sands do shift,
Creating smiles is our true gift.

So let's rewind to ancient days,
Prize-fighters in all the silliest ways.
You with a crown, and I with a cape,
In every moment, we giggle and gape.

Maps of Shared Fates

Charting the sea with crayons bright,
We sail on ships made of sheer delight.
You drew a whale, I drew a fish,
A map to treasure, or just our wish?

Every cross on this goofy chart,
Leads to a laugh, a jumpstart of heart.
In every era, we chase the same prank,
With rubber chickens and gags in the tank.

Through forests dense and mountains tall,
We trip on roots and giggle, then fall.
A compass spins with each silly tale,
In our crazy ships, we'll never pale.

So here's our map, a colorful spree,
Drawing adventures for you and me.
With crayons as stars in the midnight sky,
We sketch our fun until we fly.

The Time Between Us

Time's a jester, oh what a clown,
Ticking and tocking, upside down.
In each tick, a prank ensues,
As minute hands wear mismatched shoes.

Remember the clock that melted away?
In every age, we joyfully play.
From flip-flops to heels, we strut with glee,
Dancing through decades, just you and me.

We swap our hats from one life to next,
In every tale, a good-natured hex.
The timekeepers pine for our foolish grace,
Together we laugh in every space.

So let's toast to the moments we share,
In socks and sandals, without any care.
For in this timeline, we find our groove,
Against the clock, we'll always move.

Echoes of Two Souls

In every age, with styles so bold,
We danced like fools, stories untold.
From cavemen's grunts to the disco beats,
Our laughter rings through the time-stamped streets.

We've shared our snacks in countless forms,
In castles grand and weathered storms.
With wigs and gowns in olden days,
We found our joy in silly plays.

From rolled-up pants to funky shoes,
We pranced through life, refusing to lose.
Each moment spent, a comic scene,
As partners in crime, forever a team.

Through life we tumble, through time we glide,
With marshmallow dreams that we can't hide.
In every giggle, and every cheer,
We find the echo of you and me here.

The Tapestry of Us

Woven threads of chaos and cheer,
In every stitch, our antics near.
Time travelers in our mismatched socks,
Crafting madness where fun unlocks.

From marching bands in feathery caps,
To silent films with witty traps.
With popcorn fights and pillow wars,
We paint our world in vibrant scores.

In every era, a different game,
Like twirling dancers with a silly name.
Be it knights or astronauts we'll be,
Our joyful tune is always free.

Through every frill and every jest,
We spin our tales, we're truly blessed.
In this crazy quilt, we both reside,
With laughter stitched in every stride.

Timeless Serenade of Hearts

In ancient tunes and modern beats,
We sway and twist, not missing feats.
With lute or phone, we serenade,
In every era, our charade.

From candlelight to glow sticks' glow,
Our playful hearts just steal the show.
In ballrooms grand or backroom funk,
We share our glee, never a skunk.

In pirate ships or spaceships wide,
With creaky voices, we both collide.
We sing of plans, both wild and sweet,
With every laugh, we skip a beat.

In timeless realms, we never tire,
With jokes that spark unending fire.
From dusk till dawn, we're never through,
In every song, it's me and you.

Love's Unfading Thread

In wobbly chairs and vibrant dreams,
Our tales unfold, bursting at the seams.
From sketches rough to polished prose,
Each moment shared, nostalgia grows.

In fancy masks and goofy hats,
We craft our joy like clever brats.
With ticklish toes and goofy grins,
We rib each other, that's where it begins.

Through every workshop, every spree,
Our playful hearts are wild and free.
From silly selfies to daring stunts,
We've fashioned laughter that always haunts.

With threads of gold and hues so bright,
Our bond, a tapestry of pure delight.
In every blink and every cheer,
We're stitched together, year after year.

Together in the Cosmos

In space suits we danced, oh what a sight,
With zero gravity, we took off in flight.
Floating like balloons, giggles in the air,
Dodging asteroids with our cosmic flair.

Galaxies twinkling, we played hide and seek,
I chased you through meteor showers, oh how unique!
Your laughter echoed off distant stars,
Together forever, on our bicycles made of Mars.

Rebirth of Our Souls

We've been bees, we've been trees, so many forms,
In each life, a new way to weather the storms.
From fish in the seas to goats on a hill,
Your silly antics always give me a thrill.

In this next round, who knows what we'll be?
Perhaps cats that enjoy a nice cup of tea!
We'll prance through the ages, with giggles and grins,
In every new body, our mischief begins.

Fragments of Tomorrow's Dreams

In dreams we surf on clouds made of fluff,
Laughing so hard, we can't get enough.
We ride on the backs of whimsical whales,
Telling tall tales that are filled with detail.

Tomorrow's adventures are bright and bizarre,
Exploring new worlds, we'll secretly spar.
Playing tag with comets, our giggles like chimes,
Collecting our moments, like funny old rhymes.

Reflections in the River of Time

We skip stones in rivers, with splashes so loud,
Each ripple a memory, a joke shared with crowds.
From knights in the past to aliens green,
Every reflection shows what could have been.

In the river of time, we dance like it's spring,
Wearing silly hats and a coat made of bling.
With each little flicker, our laughter rings clear,
Together we flourish, with nothing to fear.

Notes of an Infinite Melody

In every song that's ever sung,
Our laughter dances, forever young.
Like socks that disappear in the wash,
We reunite with a silly swash.

Through fire drills and hot dog stands,
We still find joy in silly brands.
Like two clowns at a concert hall,
We share the stage, we never fall.

With hiccups and goofy grins,
Every time we start again.
Like playful tunes that spin and twirl,
We reinvent this crazy world.

In rhythms wild and fanciful,
Our friendship's truly bountiful.
From now until the end of time,
We sway and giggle, lost in rhyme.

Rewind and Replay

Click the button, start again,
A silly dance with musty men.
From pie fights to pillow wars,
We laugh, we fall, we roll on floors.

Like cartoon cats with silly hats,
We chase our dreams, just like cool cats.
Every misstep's a funny score,
In this show, we always want more.

With each rewind, we trip and skip,
As partners in this wacky trip.
A loop of giggles and sweet delight,
In time's embrace, we hold on tight.

Each replay's laced with endless glee,
Who knew this mess was meant to be?
So here we stand, absurd yet bold,
In every reel, our tales unfold.

Hearts Across the Universe

In every star that twinkles bright,
I see your grin in cosmic light.
Like wormholes made of silly dreams,
We float in space on rainbow beams.

With comets zooming, tails that twist,
We giggle through a cosmic mist.
From alien worlds with funky tunes,
We dance beneath the jiving moons.

Through each explode, a new surprise,
We're time travelers in disguise.
From Jupiter to Mars, so grand,
Our goofy hearts will always land.

So take my hand, let's fly away,
With hearts that beat in cosmic play.
In every galaxy, we find,
The wackiest love that's redefined.

The Language of Forever

In every language known to man,
Our banter flows like a silly can.
From puns to quirks, we spell it right,
Our friendship is a funny sight.

With each word twisted in delight,
We share a world that feels so light.
Like bumper cars with jingling bells,
We jabber on, our laughter swells.

Through every joke and playful jest,
We've crafted love that supersedes the rest.
In cosmic slang, we brush and tease,
Our banter drifts on the cosmic breeze.

So let's weave tales and spin our yarn,
In every moment, a joyful charm.
Forever written in the stars,
Our silly story earns its scars.

Love That Defies Dimensions

In a world of quirks and bends,
We ride the time, just two good friends.
Through space and laughs, our cheers collide,
In every era, we take a ride.

In ancient times, we led a dance,
Your clumsy moves, my sideways glance.
As dinosaurs applaud our flair,
We twirl and spin without a care.

With every laugh, we shift the stars,
From funky hats to silly cars.
In every age, a brand new scheme,
We're legends, love, or so it seems.

Across the skies, our mishaps soar,
In cosmic fairs, we ask for more.
Through every laugh and fleeting time,
We'll doodle joy in every rhyme.

Portraits Beyond a Moment

A snapshot of us, so full of glee,
Wearing mustaches, just wait and see.
With painted faces and hearts so bright,
Our moment's portrait becomes a sight.

In every frame, we strike a pose,
With silly wigs and a fake red nose.
From cavemen days, we've made a splash,
With squinty eyes, we've set the cash.

Click! Another meme for all to share,
In the gallery of our funny dare.
From pop art gems to digital space,
Nothing's more funny than our embrace.

In every moment, we boldly tread,
Creating memories that can't be said.
In frames unwound, they laugh and bend,
In every portrait, we never end.

The Stillness of Forever

In the silence that stretches wide,
We try to hide our giggling pride.
Through timeless tricks and playful jests,
We play forever, skip all the rests.

With pause and perfect timing, friend,
We freeze in frames, oh, what a trend!
In ancient tales, we share a joke,
Both of us laugh, 'till we choke.

While gods and legends watch us play,
We add our jokes to stories today.
With every wink, the cosmos grins,
And in that stillness, our joy begins.

So here's to quiet that's less mundane,
Where laughter lingers like sweet champagne.
In the vastness, let's never sever,
Each tick of time, we're funny forever.

Our Story Never Ends

In a book with pages full of cheer,
We flip the script from year to year.
With witty lines and silly puns,
Our tale unfolds in cosmic runs.

From fairy tales to epic tales,
We journey forth on laugh-filled trails.
In every chapter, we write with zest,
Finding humor, we're truly blessed.

With quirky plots and twists so bold,
Our story's woven in laughter's fold.
Through every challenge, we share a grin,
In every saga, we always win.

So as the fables twist and bend,
Remember this: our joy won't end.
In the ink of laughter, we delight,
Together, we dance into the night.

Fated Threads Through History

In a past life, we lost our way,
Chasing cats that seemed to sway.
You stole my sandwich, oh what a theft,
I named my goldfish 'Mystery Left.'

From knights in armor, to cowboys' cheer,
We've wandered together, year after year.
I tripped on a horse, it was quite a sight,
You laughed so hard, we nearly took flight.

In every age, we find some fun,
Whether we're baking or out on a run.
Like ancient jesters in a royal court,
Making mischief, of all sorts!

Through trials and errors, like a sitcom's plot,
We stand side by side, with laughter a lot.
In this endless loop, as we eternally scheme,
At the end of the day, we still joke and dream.

In the Garden of Reincarnation

In a garden of oddities, we plant our seeds,
Dancing with daisies, fulfilling our needs.
A potato dressed up as a fancy queen,
Claims it's a veggie, what a weird scene!

As tulips giggle and the daisies sway,
We whisper secrets, and frolic in play.
In this timeless plot, we skip and slide,
Climbing up rainbows, with joy as our guide.

Through generations, we swap silly tales,
Of pet frogs and treasure maps made of sails.
Each bloom remembers our laughter and cheer,
Like fine wine aging, better year by year.

In this colorful chaos, together we laugh,
Counting the smiles, as we share our path.
With every new blossom, a memory grows,
Forever entwined like a garden that knows.

Echoes of Shared Laughter

In a cozy café, we sipped our brews,
You told a joke that gave me the blues.
Spilled my cappuccino all over the floor,
We laughed so hard, I fell out the door!

In each lifetime, a sitcom unfold,
From cavement to astronauts, stories retold.
Pretending to fish with our ice cream cones,
You've always been good at crafting those puns!

In a future where robots serve our meals,
We bet on who'd win, a game of strong feels.
You chose the toaster, I picked the chair,
Turns out they're both champs; what a wild affair!

Through echoes of laughter, across every age,
Your smile's the highlight, my personal stage.
In this crazy ride, our jokes intertwine,
Life is a circus, and I'm glad you're mine!

Kin Across Eons

From cavemen drawing to future's glow,
We've battled bears and danced in the snow.
You made a spear, I fashioned my bow,
Together we laughed, as friendship would grow.

In spaceships zipping, with aliens we play,
Arguing always who's first on the day.
You claim to have won at cards last night,
I just switched your deck; what a playful sight!

From wizards to pirates, we've traveled far,
You found a treasure, but it's just a jar.
Full of old candy that tastes like regret,
Yet here we are, with no signs of fret.

In the tapestry woven, our threads are entwined,
Across every eon, our antics aligned.
With humor and joy, we light up the scene,
Partners in crime, forever serene.

Time's Gentle Embrace

In every age, a clumsy dance,
We trip and fall, what a romance!
From caveman grunts to silly cheers,
Our goofy ways span a thousand years.

With funny hats and wobbly shoes,
We take our turns, we share our blues.
Hearts collide like asteroids rare,
Through time and space, we're quite the pair.

From horse-drawn carts to rocket ships,
With snacks in hand and silly quips.
We ride the tides of fate's great whim,
And laugh aloud through every whim.

In time's embrace, we'll ever sway,
Like kids at play, we roam and play.
With every laugh, a story blooms,
Together through the world, we zoom!

Love's Eternal Quest

On treasure hunts for socks and socks,
We dodge the dragons, dance with rocks.
With maps that lead to nowhere neat,
We chase our dreams on silly feet.

Each quest begins with whispered schemes,
A kingdom built on fluffy dreams.
With knights who trip on tailcoats grand,
And jester hearts that go hand in hand.

The quest for love is full of flares,
Of tangled hair and goofy stares.
In fanciful lands where laughter reigns,
We find our way through jumbled lanes.

So here's to tales both wild and wacky,
To quests that make our hearts feel tacky.
A journey shared with joyful jest,
With you, each step is simply blessed!

Forever in Flux

In whirlwinds, we spin like leaves on trees,
With constant change that makes us wheeze.
Through wiggle worms and giggly spins,
Our twisted paths weave silly wins.

A ripple here, a bounce right there,
We leap through time without a care.
Like jello molds, we jiggle and sway,
Forever changing, come what may.

Our stories flip like pancakes hot,
With every flip, we find a spot.
New flavors swirl, a crazy mix,
With laughter as our greatest fix.

The cosmos spins, a wild ride,
With ups and downs, we laugh and glide.
Though forever in a goofy flux,
We find our way, it truly sucks!

The Harmony of Returning

With every loop, a foolish tune,
We join the dance beneath the moon.
In circles wide, we spin and twirl,
Returning like a playful whirl.

The past returns with silly tunes,
Like vintage songs that cause our swoons.
Each time we meet, we're still the same,
With added quirks to spice our game.

From past and future, we unite,
With chuckles shared on starry nights.
In wobbly hugs and tea-filled chats,
We greet each other like old cats.

This harmony of joyful rounds,
In every laugh, our friendship bounds.
With every trip and silly cheer,
We dance again, forever near!

Our Dance Through the Cosmos

In outer space we twirl and spin,
With aliens laughing, where do we begin?
Jupiter's moose joins our galactic line,
While comets throw confetti, it's party time!

Asteroids bounce like they know the steps,
We moonwalk on Saturn, well-prepped for the reps.
In a nebula, we pull off a cartwheel,
While stars wink at us, what a great deal!

Chasing stardust, we lose our way,
But every mishap just makes our day.
Planets in rhythm, what a sight to see,
In this cosmic dance, it's just you and me!

So grab your space boots, let's make a mess,
In this universe, it's all a fun guess.
We'll dance 'til supernovas go dim,
With laughter and love, we'll take every whim.

The Language of Eternal Togetherness

Whispers of giggles in every old tale,
Like cheese and crackers, we never fail.
Inventing our words, they're silly but sweet,
Puns in the air, our own private retreat.

From ancient temples to the wildest shore,
We chuckle in languages never before.
With handshakes like jazz, and winks like a song,
Together we're right where we quite belong.

In shadows of time, we write our own script,
Each punchline delivered with a playful quip.
Through ages of laughter, we banter and tease,
A cosmic connection that's sure to please!

So let's share a wink that will cross the ages,
A laugh that will echo through history's pages.
For in this grand play of the universe's show,
We're the jesters of love, just so you know!

Beneath the Endless Sky

Under twinkling stars, we set up our tent,
Roasting marshmallows, our smiles are bent.
The moon is our spotlight as we dance on the grass,
With constellations clapping, let's make this a blast!

Clouds might chuckle, as we trip and fall,
But that just adds laughter to our nightly ball.
We forget the rhythm and shimmy out of tune,
While crickets serenade beneath the lazy moon.

Our jokes bounce high, like meteors' flight,
In this night of wonders, everything feels right.
We leap through the cosmos, like stars made of glue,
In this silly adventure, it's just me and you!

So let's throw our heads back and laugh 'til we cry,
With galaxies watching, we'll reach for the sky.
In this endless night, with our hearts all aglow,
We'll dance side by side, letting all worries go.

Infinite Mirrors of Our Love

In a hall of reflections, we strike a pose,
With every turn, a new joke bestows.
Like clowns in a circus, we prance and play,
Each laugh a reminder, come what may!

Mirrors all giggle, they twist and they bend,
Replaying our mischief, around every bend.
We dance in the chaos, a silly brigade,
Creating our story, together we've made.

Our shadows are playful, they leap and they cheer,
The echoes of laughter are music we hear.
In a world of reflections, we'll play peek-a-boo,
For no matter the mirror, it's always us two!

So let's paint the town, let our spirits soar,
In this comic strip life, let's draw even more.
For every new reflection's a reason to sing,
In this whimsical journey, we've found our zing!

Mirrors of Our Journeys

In every nook, we laugh and play,
Chasing shadows, come what may.
With wigs and hats, we dance around,
A circus act we've always found.

Through time we hop, like bunnies in socks,
In each new life, we play with clocks.
You're my partner in silly crimes,
Countless pranks, in endless times.

From knights in armor, to cats in space,
Adventures we share, a wild embrace.
With every giggle, a tale unfolds,
In every age, our fun retold.

At ancient feasts, we'd toast with pie,
Invent new ways to make pigs fly.
Each lifetime's just a funny play,
Together we find our own ballet.

Harmony of Forgotten Lives

In realms of laughter, we reside,
With silly dances, side by side.
You've been my jester, I your queen,
In every age, a funny scene.

From cavemen's art to disco sway,
Our rhythm bounces through the spray.
We paint our stories, wild and bright,
With brush strokes bold, a pure delight.

As ghosts, we play in haunted halls,
Creating echoes, silly calls.
With every tick of time gone by,
We share our humor, oh so spry.

So here we laugh through every door,
In silly hats, forevermore.
In every pulse, a bond so grand,
A symphony of fun, hand in hand.

The Tapestry We Weave

In threads of laughter, stitched with cheer,
We weave our tales throughout the years.
From knights to space, with twists galore,
In every stitch, we always score.

In each new life, we play a game,
With goofy quirks, we earn our fame.
From juggling fruit to prancing dogs,
Together we laugh, through fogs and blogs.

In market squares, we burst with glee,
Selling jokes like candy for free.
With every glance, a playful wink,
In every sip, we share a drink.

From ancient plays to modern memes,
We sail on waves of silly dreams.
In every tapestry, ties so tight,
We craft our joy, pure and bright.

Always in Another Form

In every heartbeat, we collide,
With silly hats and jester's pride.
From garden gnomes to lead a crew,
We leap through time, just me and you.

In every whisper, chuckles bloom,
As we play pirates on the moon.
With treasure maps and silly scripts,
We navigate through cosmic flips.

Through every life, we share a jest,
In pizza parlors, we are blessed.
With toppings wild, we create our fable,
Making memories, if we're able.

So here we bounce, in forms anew,
From flying fish to a dancing shoe.
In each new laugh, we truly soar,
Together forever, who could ask for more?

Chords of Old Souls

We danced in a past life, oh what a sight,
A chicken and a cow, what a curious plight.
The songs we sang were a bit out of tune,
But oh, how we laughed beneath the bright moon.

In another time, we were ducks in a row,
Sailing on rivers, putting on quite the show.
With quacks and honks, we made quite the sound,
The funniest duo the farm ever found.

We played as old knights with swords that were fake,
Chased after dragons, for goodness' sake!
With our hats made of tin, and shields crafted from foam,
We ruled the jesters, and called it our home.

A lifetime ago, we were cats and their yarn,
Tangled in threads with no reason to fawn.
With a purr and a meow, in our own little dream,
Life is a joke, or so it would seem.

A Symphony of Kindred Spirits

Once we were robots, all gears and wires,
Singing off-key by some wild campfires.
With sparks flying high, we danced on old bolts,
Our laughter echoed like the silliest jolts.

Next, we were mermaids, gliding with grace,
But tripped on the seaweed, oh, what a case!
With tails all a-tangle, we splashed and we spun,
Creating a whirlpool—it was all in good fun.

In a future unknown, we're space little bugs,
Hopping through galaxies, giving each other hugs.
With antennas waving and laughter so bright,
We'll travel through stardust, what a fanciful flight!

With coffee and donuts, we're still going strong,
In every weird lifetime, we always belong.
With giggles and grumbles, we'll write our own fate,
In this fun little tale, there's no time for hate.

Guardians of Our Timeline

In ancient days, we were quite the pair,
Guarding our treasure—a long-lost hair.
A dragon was lurking, or so we would claim,
But really, we just wanted to play a new game.

Fast forward a bit, we were wizards in rags,
Casting absurd spells and swapping our tags.
With wands made of straws and goblins so cheeky,
Our magic was messy, but rarely too freaky.

In the wild west, oh what a sight,
A cowpoke and a raccoon in a ride meant for fright.
We galloped so fast, our hats flew away,
The wildest of buddies, we lived for the play!

Through every adventure, our giggles aren't shy,
From ancient civilizations to the first pie in the sky.
No matter the time, we'll always connect,
With laughter as armor, and friendship's effect.

When Time Stood Still

When clocks hit a wall and the world lost its spin,
We found ourselves grinning, let the fun begin!
We toppled the calendar, threw it aside,
With tickles and laughter, we danced like a tide.

In frozen time, we were knights in a bar,
Jousting on chairs, dreaming of fancy cars.
With cups full of soda, and snacks all around,
Our kingdom was cheesy, laughter profound.

Zoom ahead to a time when we were so bold,
Detectives in trench coats, with stories retold.
Solving great mysteries with pies on our head,
Our sleuthing was messy, and so was the bread!

When time stood still, we were full of delight,
No worries about future, just joy in the night.
In every tick-tock, we'll find something new,
In the laughs that we share, our friendship shines through.

Hearts Aligned Through Time

In ages past, we were silly twins,
Chasing each other, where fun begins.
With wigs and hats, a comical sight,
We danced through time, pure delight.

In knights' armor, we'd clash for a laugh,
You rode a horse, I took a gaffe.
In castles tall, we'd plot and scheme,
Making history feel like a dream.

Through ages of fashion, both bold and bizarre,
In every life, we raised the bar.
From flapper dresses to poodle skirts,
We reinvented our playful flirts.

So here's to us, through time so wide,
In every era, you're by my side.
We'll laugh forever, that much is clear,
In every heartbeat, I'll cheer my dear!

Destiny's Unbroken Circle

In the past, we were chickens, quite absurd,
Pecking at corn, not buzzing a word.
Through clucking chaos, we found our groove,
In dusty barns, we couldn't help but move.

Fast forward to the roaring twenties,
We opened a speakeasy – oh, so plenty!
Dressed to the nines, we served up gin,
With flapper dresses, let the fun begin.

Then came the disco, with glitter and song,
We flashed our moves, it couldn't go wrong.
Out on the floor, we danced side by side,
In sparkles and laughter, we took our ride.

So here's to the cycles that make us laugh,
In every incarnation, you'll be my other half.
Each twist of fate, a joke to unfold,
In destiny's dance, we'll never grow old!

Love's Timeless Journey

Once explorers on a silly quest,
Searching for treasures, we did our best.
With maps upside down and snacks to munch,
We laughed at our blunders while on the hunch.

In the Renaissance, we painted the town,
With colors so wild, we wore a frown!
But splashes of paint turned out to be gold,
In every artwork, our stories told.

As astronauts lost in a cosmic swirl,
We flew through stars, oh, what a whirl!
In spacesuits too tight, we floated with glee,
Creating new worlds just for you and me.

Our journey continues, with giggles ahead,
In every adventure, our silliness spread.
With each twist of fate, let's keep it light,
For love is the laughter that makes life bright!

Stars Whispers in the Dark

Beneath the stars, we played hide and seek,
In the comets' tails, we'd hide our cheek.
With twinkling eyes, we'd giggle and run,
Creating our cosmos, so much fun!

In ancient times, we rode a big whale,
Telling fish tales, we laughed without fail.
Riding the waves, we'd splash and cheer,
With salty breeze that brought us near.

Fast to the future, on hoverboards we'd zoom,
With laughter echoing, we filled the room.
Creating mischief in space age bright,
Our giggles soared higher, pure delight.

Though time may twist and life may bend,
We're comics together, it'll never end.
With stars as our witness, in every dark,
Our joy is the spark, that lights up the park!

A Path of Serendipity

In a coffee shop, we met by chance,
You spilled your drink, not quite a dance.
Your laugh was loud, I couldn't resist,
Life's odd little twist, how could we miss?

Frogs in tuxedos, we jumped that night,
Chasing our dreams, oh what a sight!
With wacky hats and mismatched shoes,
Every adventure was ours to choose.

Forgotten memories, like socks in the wash,
Each tale we share makes us both guffaw.
Through silly blunders, we find our groove,
This quirky journey has us in a swoon.

So let's raise a toast to our jester fate,
In this carnival ride, there's never too late.
With laughs and giggles, we'll twirl around,
In our own world, joy's always found.

Emblems of Our Journey

Two mismatched turtles on a sunny street,
One wears a bow tie, the other, bare feet.
We wandered the lanes, unplanned and free,
Collecting odd trinkets as happy as can be.

You painted a rock, I carved a whale,
Together we wrote our own silly tale.
Through puddles of laughter and multicolored days,
Our whimsical path is a joyful maze.

With balloons for thoughts and giggles for dreams,
We jumped over rainbows, or so it seems.
Every tumble we took became just a show,
With confetti in pockets, off we would go.

So here's to our saga of giggles and fun,
Two jolly jesters on a quest, never done.
With banners of joy and a sprinkle of cheer,
We'll keep writing stories as long as we're here.

The Unending Whisper

In a world of whispers, we seem to collide,
Like socks on a journey, we can't decide.
Chasing butterflies, or at least a kite,
Our giggles echo through the day and night.

You've got silly shoes, I've got a hat,
A recipe for laughter, just look at that!
We shimmy and shake, like leaves in a breeze,
Turning the mundane into a grand tease.

From pie in the face to slip on a floor,
Every mishap opens a new fun door.
With each strange twist, we dance and we twirl,
Life's a frisky ride in this zany whirl.

So let's float on clouds of giggly delight,
With hearts full of jests and spirits so bright.
Through roundabouts of humor, we'll sprint,
Each laugh a reminder, our hearts never tint.

Ink on Time's Canvas

With crayons in hand, we scribble our dreams,
A masterpiece painted with laughter and beams.
You drew a giraffe who wears funky specs,
While I sketched a shark, in polka dot checks.

In the park, we danced on a rainbow slide,
Each loop and each twist sends our giggles wide.
Kites whoosh above, in all hues they glide,
Our palette of joy, on time's wild ride.

Through pranks and mishaps, we write our own book,
Each chapter a chance for a whimsical look.
With splashes of color and doodles of cheer,
Our canvas expands as we revel nearer.

So let's paint this life with the brightest of hues,
With each laugh we share, we never lose.
For in this gallery, our spirits soar high,
Creating a world where we both can fly.

Reincarnations of Connection

In each new form, we joke around,
A cat, a dog, we're glory-bound.
Every lifetime, a quirky twist,
From ancient lands to the modernist list.

With hats and capes, we play the game,
Each time we meet, it's never the same.
You laugh, I snort, we dance with glee,
From pharaohs to jesters, just wait and see.

In one life, a knight with a steed,
In another, a chef, oh what a deed!
We bond through chaos and matching socks,
Rediscover each other in cosmic blocks.

So here's to the lives where we trip and fall,
With smiles and giggles, we conquer it all.
Through every age and every plot,
It's a comical script we can't stop!

Embracing Spaces Between Us

In every distance, a chuckle's born,
From spaced-out planets to sleepy corn.
We text from afar with memes so fine,
And share our laughs like bottles of wine.

Across the void, I wink and shout,
"Where's my sandwich? What's that about?"
In every pause, a magic spree,
Your face in pixels, and oh so free.

In past lives, we'd ride on clouds,
In silly outfits, oh how we'd crowd.
Every gap, a playful tease,
Whispering jokes on the cosmic breeze.

So here's to the spaces, vast and wide,
Filled with laughter on this joyride.
No matter the distance or funny plight,
We'll always find ways to delight.

Footprints on the Sands of Time

With sandy toes, we trek this shore,
Leaving giggles in waves that roar.
Each footprint tells a story true,
Of silly things I did with you.

In centuries past, we built our dreams,
From sandcastles to ice cream streams.
The tides come in, but laughter stays,
In each bizarre twist of our playful days.

Through every age, we scribble fun,
Chasing the seagulls, oh what a run!
With each sunset, we turn to play,
Marking moments in a hilarious way.

So let the tides rise and fall as they might,
We'll dance through the dusk and into the light.
In every grain, our fun will climb,
Laughing together, one laugh at a time.

Celestial Dance of Us

In cosmic waltz, we spin around,
With starry giggles that know no bound.
From twinkling lights to planets red,
We laugh together, like peanut butter spread.

In a galaxy far, we've shared a pie,
And high-fived comets as they whizzed by.
We joke with aliens, play hide and seek,
In this vast universe, we're never weak.

Through black holes and stripes, we zoom in glee,
With every swirl, it's just you and me.
We twirl through star dust, like popcorn in flight,
Creating fun stories, every night.

So let's joyride through the starry sky,
With laughter and joy, we leap and fly.
In this celestial dance, we take our stand,
Forever entwined, hand in hand.

www.ingramcontent.com/pod-product-compliance
Ingram Content Group UK Ltd.
Pitfield, Milton Keynes, MK11 3LW, UK
UKHW020122171224
452675UK00014BA/1524